SLOW PHOENIX

Poems by

Michael Favala Goldman

Cyberwit.net
HIG 45 Kaushambi Kunj, Kalindipuram
Allahabad - 211011 (U.P.) India
http://www.cyberwit.net
Tel: +(91) 9415091004
E-mail: info@cyberwit.net

Printed at Thomson Press India Limited.

DEDICATION

This book is dedicated to:
Benny Andersen, Knud Sørensen, and Marianne Koluda Hansen
three outstanding Danish poets
who permitted me to translate their books
which helped me to find my own voice in poetry.

ACKNOWLEDGMENTS

I am grateful to the following journals for first publishing these poems:

Silkworm: "The Contract," "Balance," and "The Bee Game"

Meat for Tea: "Trust Burns," "What I tell myself," and "The Reprieve"

Common Ground: "Water"

The Fourth River: "Late winter, potting"

The Aurorean: "Cold"

Stoneboat: "Slow Phoenix"

Borderlands: Texas Poetry Review, "Ammonius"

PREFACE

Dear Reader,
Poetry has an interesting relationship with time.

Poetry can freeze a moment so it can be looked at
from various angles, then be shared, be experienced
vicariously, analyzed or felt, and shared again
with people perhaps far removed from the author.

Poetry can become conversation across time,
regardless of time, taunting and thwarting time,
which otherwise whisks moments quickly away

Poetry can add a sense of eternity.

Keep the conversation going.

Michael Favala Goldman
Florence, MA
May, 2021

Contents

3

4

1

You ought to read Benny Andersen

On the occasion of Benny Andersen's 82nd birthday

Soft words crumble on the page
commaclink
periodmumble
babbleclamor
the man's giftgrumble
sound of distant rubber memories
anthologies are being filled
phrases slide close by one another
the air noonsour from declinations
stimulations
overturned tea-cozies

You ought to read Benny Andersen
brush off the bills and the remote
look up something
embark
dash out to the library with rolled-up soul
library without grades
without card
without delay
you ought to get involved
in a short wild now associate with researchers
philologists
and nearly overheard children
and in between undertake dynamic purchasing of
humaneness dilemmas and wonder
come to laugh

to grow silent
come to
eventually lose your inner bowler hat
you ought to read
not just the poem
the point
the portent
you ought to ought to

or you ought to rest first
you have the book in front of you
the chair behind you
still have old children's rhymes in your ears
you ought to gather strength
rest intensely
perplexedly
hold your tongue
the connection
the book
proceed heedlessly into the poetry like a specter
hurl all your noon-appointment impulses into your briefcase
and quivering prepare to recognize yourself

Benny Andersen (1929-2018) is the all-time, best-selling poet in Denmark.

The Little Cinema

Love's arrow tip slips into
the narrowest circumstance

Hemingway wrote a book
Which became a movie
Advertised on a marquee
In a small city in Denmark

I thought I'd like to see that film
Everyone else had plans
That last night of summer
In Silkeborg, 1983.

Your mother suggested you go along
With me but you resisted
She offered her car, and to pay
So you gave in.

I was distraught –
You were the most gorgeous girl
Taking me to the movies
Your boyfriend was huge.

Fiat made the smallest car
Green with the loudest engine
The worst ambience
In four speeds.

The theater was even smaller
The film projected on the back
Of my eyes. The seats so close
We oscillated.

Ever since the lights came on
Gary Cooper and I
Have been inseparable
Protecting you from the war.

Frankfurt Terminal

Looks like the race is on
between the gray-haired man
(the one wearing the green Hawaiian shirt,
cream-colored pants and gray rubber shoes,
holes showing white socks)
and the female employee riding the floor sweeper

She's focussed on the baseboard
and how the rotating bristles
converge with the corner
while he's shuffling, staring
just below the horizon of the long walkway

She has to veer around the aluminum trash barrels
with their international symbols for bottles and refuse
and then again
around the seating area to not disturb the patrons eating

She gains on the straightaway
He doesn't have a chance.

Ode to an exhaust fan

Conflation
of simple machines
rudimentary robot
replacing drudgery
of ancient slaves
with simple fins spinning
obeying currents
encased in copper
creating currents –
middle-thing
ace-in-a-hole
air tender
voiding remains of
densities needing dilution
draft encourager
single-minded servant
clearing clouds
dispersing damp
obviating vapor
everyday in motion
with switch and dial
worldly whirling
sending accumulated atoms
into receiving space:
your quintessence –
our renewal.

Free to enter New Jersey

Arteries from the north
sweep across bridges
through clouds of sickening aromas.
From the west more bridges –
New Jersey is an island,
trying to erase its borders,
making it imperceptible
where city ends and you
begin. From the south a memorial
to how many plunged
into wet concrete
immortalized in pillars
holding up your dash
to flat monachopsis
which is the feeling of being
in the wrong place.
From the east simply float
to overpopulated docks.
Greet this fragmented land
with family, maybe
a funeral. It will cost you plenty
to get out again.

Ode to Floss

I never realized
there are so many kinds
of dental floss
different shapes and coatings
cinnamon, cardamom, micro mint
whatever that is
different delivery schemes
disposable plastic stirrups, mini-nunchucks
thumbchucks
cases with colorful accents
each with their own tiny metal cutter
actually
I never used to floss
but my dentist scared me into it
so I bought some
and ended up with 50 yards of a kind
I don't like at all.
Sometimes
I look for poems
really in the wrong places.

One by One

at 121 Club

It was Wayne Shorter's birthday
which was so great
since we were going to perform one
of his compositions at the jazz club
made it all kind of fortuitous –
to tell the audience we were playing for him
the groovy intro, the quiet melody and
the shouting notes that maybe he could sense somehow
and our improvisations on his tune
each of us having a minute for his life to step
specter-like into ours and us shouting from his mountaintop
that this, *this* is what it feels like
to have been Wayne Shorter as a young man
and even though he's 83 he still feels it
and his music still plays it
that way and there's no regret or sadness
when it's played like that – just the sounds
flooding the walls and reflecting off the bright
upturned faces, and after the applause
I thank the audience, defer to Shorter's birthday
again and it doesn't matter that I say Frank
Shorter by accident that time, because when I was young
my family was really into long-distance running
and our saxophonist corrects me and
we're on to the next tune.

The Man in White

In memory of Djembe Charles

I walked past the carriage house,
old housemate,
still hear echoes of your class,
West African rhythms in ensemble,
children and adults, learning from you,
though your djembe stands alone now.

Languid Michigan city boy,
at first I looked down on you,
your patience confounded me,
like when it took you all summer to paint our house
with even, four-inch brushstrokes,
the brush still nearly new
after three coats.

Sometimes I was exasperated, I admit,
by the time you finished weeding a bed
or got to the point
or hinted that an opinion lurked
beneath your tolerance.

Brother in white, you walked the hill road
every morning in every weather,
taught me to carry a switch
for horseflies. I still do this.

Eventually we learned one another's rhythms
by heart, how to relate to them, how to listen,
and in the end, to marvel.

The session is over now.
Drummers, bell and xylophone players
laid down their mallets
and spilled into the street
bearing your rhythms with them.

My heart is gently beating.
Ah, my good friend,

there you are.

San Francisco

From the next table:
When you take ecstasy
does it make you feel
sexual?
An Asian waitress arrives
with my plate a heaping
masterpiece
half-dome of crystal bean sprouts
just plucked from their hydroponic womb
strewn Pollack-like across a steaming mound
of flat noodles decorated with frill-edged carrot suns,
half-cooked cabbage shreds,
seared egg nuggets and fried tofu squares,
bordered with ground roasted peanuts served
with a quarter lime.
I feel like I almost don't deserve
the good fortune of happening to enter
this restaurant as I wandered the city street
near my hotel. I can see why the dining room is packed
with echoing conversation and the National League
wild card game on TV (which this city's team
will go on to win) which prodded me to sit here
out front by the sidewalk where women in black leather boots
and young mop-haired men walk their bicycles
while I squeeze the bitter juice across my dish
and squint through the glass at the score

News

For twenty years we never got a paper
or watched the news
but recently we subscribed

we like the option
of skimming
selected world surfaces

over breakfast
see national policy
takes up the same space
as pureed soups and
the football draft

even after turning over all the pages
it still lies quite flat
as if muttering
to itself

Nlobesse'e, Cameroon

Outside the school
hundreds of patients asleep
on the ground with their families

In the middle of the night
a bus of medical volunteers arrives

Three tables in a bare room
no door in the door opening
no windows in the windows

For children sedatives
adults local

Hernias repaired
tumors removed
for ten hours

Each gets a bag of Tylenol
to take home

Enough

Poetry relocates suffering

onto a page

Who really needs to know
how bad things have been?

Aren't there enough calls
for help?

If poetry is trying to soften
one heart

at a time

so some day
there will be no tolerance
for the misery of others

Well

okay then.

Neighbor's Wife

White felt hat
no smile on my stoop
red-rimmed eyes

I say Come in.
Do you want to sit down?

I pull out a chair
It stays empty.

Since you live so close
I just read the report
It's brain cancer
They said it's the worst kind
I can't stay long

Black leather footsteps
down the walk just cleared
of heavy, wet snow.

Compassion

A break from driving
lounging on a patch of grass

A couple arrives in a truck
sits down nearby

He embraces her aggressively
makes me wonder

He has silver teeth
wiry hair

He pulls out a little tool
stabs his belly, then injects something

He turns to me, says,
"What're you looking at?"

Throws his waste at me
it sails by

I say, "Well,
you did sit right next to me."

We all get up.
To the young woman, I say,

"You can get into my van
if you need to get away."

A brief pause, then
she strides over to my vehicle
sits down inside

I start it
The man steps up outside
holding on at my window

He's speaking, trying
to convince her to stay

I want to shake him off
so gently he doesn't get hurt.

2

Wear

My current winter coat
I bought at a yard sale.
It's gotten dingy now, and a patch on one arm
keeps in the feathers.

I imagine coats on an assembly line
getting zippers and pockets,
tags and logos,
each coat identical, as designed,

replicas all the way down. One of these
will be hanging in a shop
when I arrive and it will fit
so well I'll buy it, so perfectly

mass-produced to protect
from the elements this person,
singularly worn,
all the way through, in places.

Water

The heart's pericardium
membrane aches like hell if you stretch it
all the way to Chicago.
Nothing against The Second City
or the terrific Russian restaurant there
off Michigan where we had our last
dinner and all the waiters incessantly
filled our water glasses.
Good for the heart, drinking water
till it leaks out the eyeballs
lowering our salt which they say
is also good. My heart stretches all on its own.
Though it hurts, I want it to.

Lost Wax

All my soft places
crave dissolving,
but I need more heat
molten metal
pouring into me
filling folds
cauterizing
giving weight
substance enough
to persist

Devil's Tower, late afternoon

Tramping behind you on the desert trail
crisp basalt litter to both sides
molts of this enormous obelisk
how I hated you

you were far too good
hiding behind your naive smile
as if goodness could save anything
as if defenselessness could keep you
from hurting me

show me your teeth!
however white and straight they may be

Tramping in the dust
obliterating sand swirls in the shadow
of this primeval monolith
erect and tilting
still shedding cool brokenness.

Trust Burns

Trust burns
on the way out

ignites the fuse
dry and white
in my core

consumes
a dizzying path down

Ashes on the ground
hide an angry glow

don't you dare
blow on it

Grief

Without intending to
I downed a whole bottle
of limoncello

I had walked into the store
It occurred to me
they had it – your favorite

Tossed back
in time
I am grateful

Looking ahead
You're no longer there
except what is left
at the bottom of me

I drink to you

feel how
you almost
disappear

Flicker

Arriving home from your island
pulling in after the long flight
a good-sized dead bird
lies in front of the garage door
I get out of the car
notice
the flame feathers hidden
under grey wings

Audubon confirmed my suspicions
a flicker
bird you loved above all others
flash in the forest you pointed to
the call you bade me hear
and imitate
thirty years ago

Does it matter
you were married
two young children
when we walked into the woods
me reciting poetry
narrating the story of my loves
my life less than half
yours in years

Does it matter your dark hair
hung to your waist
your long midwestern body
bent over the moveable type

as we laid letters of some unpublished poet
at your living room press

Or that when I had to
leave the island
in my hand-painted car
you threw in your lot with mine
released yourself temporarily
from wifehood and motherhood
to expiate a great unspoken
suffering
on a Black Hills peak

Does it matter that
I bobbed your hair
after you lopped it off sobbing
over the flickering ceremonial fire
or that we sat for Wild West
portraits in costume
frozen in time

Does it matter that we slept
in a cave
traversed edges of a primeval
pairing
before the shock of
Fargo Airport
where tears released you
back
into your life

Does it matter that I helped
my father build his house
next to yours

where the road dead-ended
at the forest
that years later on my irregular visits
I would see your road
but never you

My family and I flew to your island
to visit him.
The day before we left
we stood out front talking
you walked by with your dog

We waved you over
in the cool weather you shook
all our hands. I greeted
your dog. Some words indicated
some more words. You had to get home.
Your hat made it impossible to gauge
the length of your grey hair

I sit quietly now
with the dead flicker
at the base of a tree in our woods
on the other side of this country
At last I leave it to nature's
myriad fates except
for one plucked feather. For this

I fashioned a cork disc
with a hole into which I placed
the yellow shaft. To this day
it stands by my bed
a flame of flight and mystery.

To one who has lost touch

Tell me you never got the gift certificate I sent you
    or that you didn't know who it was from

Tell me I wrote or said something
    that left you with a sour taste

Tell me I'm too enthusiastic
    too much trouble

Tell me you've stopped talking to all your friends
    because your marriage has gotten really bad
        or really good

Tell me you're studying so hard
    you have no energy to lift a finger

Tell me time has become irrelevant to you
    so there's no need to stay in touch

Tell me I should stop thinking about you
    because you have taken on an unmentionable habit

Tell me you've been really sick

Tell me you never liked me in the first place.

Let's Play: The Bee Game

All the males lumber around the house or
hang out on the porch
getting fed by the females
and growing fat and lazy
The males are harmless
If they get excited all they can do
is make loud droning noises
Their only job is
in the spring to fly up and have sex
in mid-air with the queen
who rips out their penis and they drop dead
The unsuccessful drones hang out till winter
when the females throw them out
to die in the cold

Meanwhile all the females, except the queen,
are workers who tend to the males
and also to thousands and thousands of eggs and babies
keeping them warm, fed and cosy
in tiny rooms made of wax flakes
which the females peel from their bellies
On nice days they fly to thousands of flowers
wearing down their wings
to provide food for everyone
They don't like to be disturbed
and are quick to defend
Females have stingers
but if they use them, they die

Post-Virtue

I have given up
trying to be good

Whatever goodness I had
I leave be
so I don't mess it up

Better
to not ruffle feathers
make my life harmless

Leave me alone.

I've decided

You don't match
the items on my list

But I've decided to let you
adore me more
than I really want

I've cleared a narrow space
in my closet

I am inuring myself
to cutting back
on my solitude

Creation

All I see
hear
touch
taste
smell
is registered
on the sense volutes
inside my brain
And my entire life sensorial
is occurring there
though I have gotten quite accustomed
to perceiving it as all outside myself

If it weren't for me
you would not exist

Status Quo

I don't give you the attention
you deserve

You are a periphery
while you speak

I admire your shape
wonder when I might get lucky

I pay attention
to the you I have created

You go on as if
we're on the same page

The Special Date

Take a look
in my picnic basket:
	blanket and wine
	goat cheese and figs
	quinoa salad and grapes;

and under that –
an abyss:
	insecurity and misogyny
	blended with sex fantasies.

All this I prepared.

Go ahead.

Take it out.

Blue

matches nothing
in my house
but your eyes
as you sit
on my brown couch
examining me
making me want
to devolve
into a creature
with fewer organs

Growth

Sometimes
it seems like
every other sentence
out of my wife's mouth
indicates
a growth opportunity
for me
and I don't mean
the kind
of growth opportunity
that I'm
thinking about
if you know what I mean
yet in that moment
I get the sense
that the two
are inextricably
linked.

After a shower

You grip your baby-blue bath towel
in your teeth
so it drapes down
covering one and a half breasts
your belly your patch of hair
and half the longitude
of your legs
This way you can gather up
your long tresses
in your hands behind your head
elbows raised
to wring out the water
Without a word
I remove the towel from the grip
of your teeth
and using just one square inch
start drying your skin
beginning at one shoulder
you raise your arm
I'm in no hurry
You have to go to work
but we are both working
on a silence too strong to break
I pat down your breasts
and in small arcs across your waist
You turn around
Your back a plain
after a gentle rain
where I lie down

staring all morning
at the blue sky
and dissipating clouds

Double happiness

The windows of our skin open

two nearly starless nights commingling

voids unveiled.

Alter Ego

My spirit overlaid with a woman's
I see her when my eyes close
her thin fingers within my stubby ones
her smooth belly under mine
her pale eyelids half open, she observes
with a fertile bearing, touches
my lover more gently
than I ever could, and with no
thought of return. Her animal-like
attention. The skin all along her body.
She inhabits me, softens
my encounters, receives
without craving more.

Not enough to be young and beautiful

We were once
desire and fear overflowing
transcendence and brokenness tottering
through our days
nights together

Waking up
Waking up

Slow as aging

This moment is an age
calling home all our ages –
the transparent yous and mes
dwelling beneath our skin

Balance

The line between the yin and the yang

Swirling concave and -vex, inside and out, time and space

The interfacc

Between you and me

Where we meet and do not intrude

Equilibrium

Before blaming, before laughing

Before change

It must be

Just the way it is

The Contract

I will make you miserable for years
You will make me miserable for years

I will love you despite this
You will love me despite this

I will blame myself for hurting you
You will blame yourself for hurting me

Though it wasn't my fault
Though it wasn't your fault

I will be patient while you are lost
You will be patient while I am lost

I will take the journey back to myself
You will take the journey back to yourself

In the distance I will see you waiting for me
In the distance you will see me waiting for you

3

Cold

I get cold easily
yet I married a Nordic woman
and we live where the winters are long

I've discovered a void in my youth
a blank record
of years with no tenderness

So I wear a wool hat
inside if I have to
and consider skiing punishment

I go ice fishing
in the hole of my childhood
reel in
empty hooks

My Parents

My mother is a yellow butterfly
She died in a car crash when I was nineteen
I don't see her very often

My father survived the crash
and another
and drinking himself to death
and getting shot by a shotgun
finally succumbed to heart failure
which I guess he had all along

Now he's a butterfly bush
which dies back every winter
then grows dozens of purple flower spikes

Cold Harvest

I felled a grandfather
oak that stood
at the edge of the bog
losing limbs

Earth-bound anger crashed
I struggled with the heavy rounds
skidding them over frozen ground
uphill groaning like a beast

I hacked my memories
into pieces stacked them
neatly, their round eyes
staring at the rainy spring woods

Next winter I will warm myself
with this cold harvest
light the emptiness
reduce it to ashes

Raptor

her large-orbed eyes survey the field
glimpse me flinching
I'm not really alive until a second later
in her talons
her tearing at my organs with her beak
my shapeless wounded things
mine, but I won't admit it
inclined to cower, but
in her clutches
finally feeling kinship

Jaws

Between vertebrae 4 and 5
I harbor a springed hinge
with a serrated jaw

held open by preoccupations
and fear of being found out
as an imposter
so I'm careful about bending
and overreaching

In lucid moments I live
from my hips
a bear cub frolicking
in a compost pile
or ambling through a green corridor

one mis-step
and the old iron clamps shut

January

A deep snow fell in the night
too much to deal with

but as the hours pass
inescapable

might as well
start digging

don't think about how long
how much

better how crystalline
how phenomenal

small movements
advancing steps

wind and gravity
shadows and shapes

come upon
a path revealed

Late winter, potting

It is zero degrees out
and I am filling my seed trays
I have sent off the queries
and manuscripts
to places even colder

There's twenty inches of rimy snow outside
hard enough to dent one's ideals
Inside I handle dry soil
individual seeds
that have lain patiently in their paper
waiting
They think spring is coming

It is all they think of

I level the soil knowing
that without me
there is no hope for them

Even with me
their future
looks precarious

Clearing the Lot

It's nothing
for a large machine
rumbling shaking the air
rolling slowly on enormous black tires
hydraulic fluid veins under pressure
joints greased
to lift its bucket arm
according to delicate movements of pudgy fingers
from within the glass cabin
then to press bucket to coarse bark
of vibrant oak chestnut
and a footsole lowers the worn steel plate
opposes the spring mechanism to the floor
so the engine roars like a bull
straining against an ancient yoke
and slowly tilts the life of a century
roots stretching and snapping
losing its hold on the earth, leaning
to unfamiliar horizontal
and the shrill engine noise retreats
the bucket arm retracts, lowers
ready for more

The Reprieve

When the damp strips of cast-off bark lie slack
like leather tongues on the old boundary stone wall
and the rabbit tracks leave an icy staccato in the snow
I tire of myself
sitting hours at my desk
and let myself be drawn by the cold hazy sun
out into the pathless woods
where stout trees stand half-dressed
draped in damp moss to the north
but bare to the south in half-naked anticipation.
There is a place where water seeps slowly past to the bog
with stones large enough for stepping
and a single Japanese multiflora rose sinks its thorns into my coat
as I walk by to enter the stand of white birches.
Nearby are vernal pools
charted by my weekend hiking partner
who photographed and registered the sites
when he got wind of a developer
who was going to build eighty-four houses here.
Past the birches the soils get sandier
there below the snowcover
just perfect for the endangered Eastern Box turtles
who plod around there
some with expensive radio antennae
so the developer might know
where he may and may not dig.
I recall the neighborhood meeting
earlier this week
when the town planner announced

that all these woods
and the bog too
and the vernal pools
and the turtles
had been purchased by the city
as conservation land
except for a handful of building lots
out on the edge along the road
all this would remain more or less
as it is now
and I wonder if anyone told the land
it was given a reprieve
or if I were the first –
that the turtles can relax
the coyotes and toads
can count on returning
to their hunting and breeding grounds
another season
the saplings can continue to stretch
in the shadows of their giant forebears
and when I tire of myself
and this great disjointed world
threatens to pull me apart with it
I will still be able to slip off to this place
where the strips of bark lie slack on the stones
and the damp moss clothes the sturdy trees.

Gardening

There is something calming
about following the movements of generations

creating furrows
bending to sow, cover and tamp.

Fate, like weather
has numerous permutations –
Don't get stuck on one outcome.

I don't even imagine one bean forming –
then there's generous space for devotion
when the vines are dripping with them.

Some years everything goes wrong.
Dead plants don't respond to anger.
I look to improving the soil.

September

In the woods this morning
I saw several low branches
spread wide with yellow leaves
which surprised me

I know it's September
which is not a summer month here
but why the rush?

The sun is still warm enough
to wilt weeds by afternoon,
we're still sleeping naked
with all our windows open

From the forest edge the seeds of brush
float away as tiny ghosts.

Mortality

For me to be alive
lots of things have to die
so I try to reduce my death footprint
go vegan
barefoot
stay home
so that life has less reason
for revenge.

Vermont Moonlight

The bay is breathing
Tethered boats rise and fall
No one is going anywhere

4

Natal

My mind is the nature
of a baby deer still unlicked
perceiving the blurred woods
as yet unaware
of collecting its long limbs
yearning only to suckle
at a nameless mother

Blindness

I used to have an innate belief
in the future:

my talent would rise
like a bright moon.

Then memory woke me
to regret:

now I'm trying to believe
in the past.

Lineage

I am a fool
for taking so long
to realize exactly that

Even this
will not deter me

I will follow
in the great tradition
of fools before me

Rehabilitation

There is no determination so prized
that it can stand in the way
of craving

No power so sacred
it can't be destroyed
in the name of satisfying

No way of life so justified
it can corral conscience
to suffer a new beginning

Anachronist

I am analog at heart.
My display does not glow.
In a chamber, intrepid gearworks
chew the used seconds.
I tremble at times –
age, alarm, inertia.
Entropy accumulates
imperceptibly
slowly
winding
me
down.

Discipline

Your mind is distraction
a baby wanting your attention

It is always crying
and you care, you're compelled

This may seem coarse
but try letting it go for a while

Eventually it will calm down
when it realizes you're not coming

Ammonius

For ten years I have sat in this desert
one book
cloudless sky
sand between my toes
pitcher half full
days like dates
sweet and uniform

I don't know if I am seeking God
or hiding from Him
I sit watching the line
where the sand meets the sky

More than anything
I want to want less –
just this fraction of world
minus exotic dreams
just these few fruits
simple shelter
thin gospel

May my attention someday become whole
single
unreeling
like a silk thread
pulled from a cocoon.

Ammonius the Hermit was a 4th-century Christian ascetic and the founder of one of the most celebrated monastic communities in Egypt.

Tenzo

The pantry ingredients –
Just enough

Every grain cared for

This task
turns the cosmos.

The Tenzo is the head cook in a zen monastery.

5

The Canvass

If your one last need
was to improve the world
a little
would you pursue all your silences
until you came upon
the fearful legacy lodged inside
or would you start knocking
on your neighbor's doors
admonishing them to be good?

Jante

*The grownups think they are teaching us the difference between good
and bad. What they actually are implanting in us is something different:
They are taking revenge on us for their own childhood.*
  - Aksel Sandemose

I turned to face faces
one after another
seeking closeness

Found only distance of many kinds:
Confusion, sternness, animosity

Finally got used to it,
learned their language
without ever aspiring to

It was all there was, dammit.

*Note: Jante (pronounced 'Yanta') is the fictitious name Sandemose uses
for the town of his, and anyone's, childhood.*

Emotions 101

I walked into the classroom
and the teacher asked
"Are you feeling anything?"
And I said,
"I don't think so…"
and she said to have a seat.
When people were settled she started
by saying there were five main emotions:
anger, sadness, shame, fear and joy
and I raised my hand and asked why
only one of them was good
and she gave me a look
that probably was meant for me to feel
something in the ashamed category
but actually I felt
kind of righteous
which seemed to me
more in the happy category.
The great majority in the class were male
and I wondered what equivalent class
would draw mostly women
to look at their deficiencies.
And the teacher said for us to close our eyes
breathe deeply and
imagine our bodies
and any tensions we feel
and that maybe as we sense those tensions
maybe we could feel some kind of emotion
on the list up front.

I felt a little sad
that I could have been fishing
instead of sitting inside
on a day like this
and then I spaced out for a bit
and someone started talking
about how they were bullied
by their older brother
back when they were kids
which reminded me
about being harassed by my sister
when I was little
which is kind of awkward to admit
but she was unusually tough for a girl
and maybe she did only do it
because we were both neglected
and any attention, even being punished
was better than nothing.
But from my vantage point
I just felt sad
that my only sister didn't love me
which left pretty much no one.
When I started listening again
the teacher was asking everyone
to imagine their hearts expanding
to make room for all the feelings.
Then she recited some kind of prayer
that signaled the end of class.

I guess it was alright.

Indignant

May I file a complaint?

I was not raised
in a reasonable environment

Not that I blame anyone
particular

but was any thought put into this?

Sabbath, with ancestors

We two sat at sabbath dinner
lit a large braided candle
invited our ancestors to join us
they crowded in

we sang sabbath prayers with them
the flame swayed and smoked
we sent them light
they shed light on us

we drank to them
they admonished us
to partake of sweetness

we broke bread with them
without them

the flame was hungry
we were hungry

you reached for the skillet
knocked the candle into the curry
tipped over your glass
we dried our cheeks

the flame was adamant
spewing soot into the air
ashes floated above our meal

the smoke alarms sounded
we set up fans
opened doors to the frigid night

the alarms screeched in fits
we held hands
our breath

finally had to banish the candle
to the winter void
watch it blaze
through the window

Reminder

Just being cheerful
is hard enough
just being cheerful

I have to remind myself
about the light of the world
I have to remind myself

To live each day
with no regrets
To live each day

Just to show it's possible
fill out my skin
just to show it's possible

Regardless of success
dedicate my life
regardless of success

Planting garlic with my dad

There have been a couple of light frosts
but nothing to worry about
when you join me willingly
through the creaking gate to help plant
my cache of cloves before the year gets too late.

The cover crops have come up beyond mere stubble
on the patches where produce once
was harvested in full baskets before breakfast.
Now you are sixty-nine, in clean pants, having never
done this before. Sharing the shovel, I show you
how deep, how close we have to dig.
You bend to the hole momentously, asking
of the pointed white wedge, "Which side goes down?"

Despite my kitchen's misgivings,
I have always set aside my most select, stoutest cloves
for annual planting, believing that from them their future
generations will punctually form,
become ever more muscular and pungent and finally
be lifted in their fragile parchments when I have waited
the winter through. Together now, we seal the roots
into their accustomed darkness.

Faith

A moment in a conversation
feeling the earth turn one quiver
and there is this honest speech
lying on my tongue
like milkshake
and I'm not sure
if it's how I really feel
or if it were placed there

Instead of swallowing
I speak
what I didn't even know
and am hearing for the first time
I sense my mouth moving
and the reaction
of the listener
is more
than the usual.

To one who got into
the master's program of her choice

The streetlight changes
Daughters run with their book bags
Sunshine glares from half-behind a building
    so I have to shield my eyes
Jazz concert tonight at The Wheelhouse
Paper airplanes
First steps into the bright silent kitchen
Warm golden toast
108 seedlings just sown in their cups

Today everything
is dedicated
to you

Slow Phoenix

Sometimes I feel resentful
about having my problems

but as the days pass
and I don't burst into flames
I'm thinking

I have just enough problems
to keep me moving

What I tell myself

Pick no fights;
defeat the inner mind of contention.

Perception
is a mirror.

Before blaming,
resolve inconsistencies.

Achieving resolution,
the world becomes natural.

Don't trip up
on expectations.

When you are done
go home.

Victory

I want his team to lose
over and over and over
so he loses interest
and turns back to my silence

I want to show an interest
know the players
how long the game lasts
why they do those things

I want to lock him away
have the run of the place myself
try and remember
why I'm here in the first place

I want his team to win
so he'll be happy

Proud parent. The exodus.

I'm washing dishes and crying into the god-damned sink, scraping fucking cheese off of the toaster oven tray, after my son's burrito, which is his favorite food and he's probably 80% made of burritos and it was the last tortilla in the fridge and he's leaving for college on Saturday.

Three weeks ago I moved my older son to Chicago and when we were packing the truck it occurred to me that I had helped him to make most of his furniture. I couldn't even remember making some of the stuff, but there it was anyway, reminding me of the years when he would pester me about doing things and not go away until I did what he wanted. Kids can be a real pain in the ass.

And I'm no furniture maker, I'm a writer who used to be a carpenter. And I packed that truck as carefully and tightly as I could and drove that god-damned 12-foot skateboard 1000 miles and set him up with a springboard to a new life that I'm really fucking proud and excited about. But now all I see in my mind is us crying on each other's shoulders in his god-damned totally adequate white kitchen and I'm going to miss him because he forced me not to miss what it means to be a father.

The weeks before he moved he kept calling us up and inviting himself over for dinner, and coming over to hang out and help with my house projects. Now my other son has been baking pies and cakes for me all week and cooking up lunches and dinners with his usual flair. And leaving me the fucking dishes.

Rules

State any rule
with a smile

don't take it
too seriously

Just that twitch
a few millimeters

preserves
  childhoods
friendships
wilderness

Horizon

Do not worry about a thing
once it is done –
there are enough swamps in the world
for sinking,
enough small damp creatures
churning the muck
and clouded water.
Do not occupy yourself
with movements subterranean.
Become the horizon
it's curved razor slicing the sky.
All answers are there
on that edge of pain and light.

Knock knock

Get up
go to the door
and greet your life
like a cousin
you haven't seen
for a long time.

Invite him in.
You have a lot in common.

You have a lot
of catching up to do.

www.ingramcontent.com/pod-product-compliance
Lightning Source LLC
La Vergne TN
LVHW051453170726
843492LV00002B/669